MW00884579

From the Ashes

An Individual's Journey from Bullied, Destroyed, and Ultimately Reborn to a Life of Purpose, Joy, and Power

Dr. J. Fitzgerald Alexander, DBA, MBA, BS

Owner of J. Xander-Cole Limitless, LLC

Anti-bullying Advocate, Keynote Speaker,

Leadership Mentor, Performing Strongman

ISBN-10: 1721638539
ISBN-13: 978-1721638536

DEDICATION

Success never occurs in a vacuum. Bill Clinton once stated that if you ever see a turtle on the top of a fence post, you can be certain that he had help getting there. There are so many people who pave the way for us and walk with us side by side. There is no way that I would be the man, academic or leader that I have grown into without the love and support of my two favorite ladies. My wife Lora Renee Alexander, and Joselyn Faith Alexander have been with me at pivotal points in my life while enduring my brand of crazy. I could not have taken on this project and written this manuscript without both of you being here. My family has always been my biggest fans, and this book is dedicated to you.

CONTENTS

July 2016 at my commencement with my two Favorite Ladies: My daughter Joselyn on the left and My Wife Renee on right.

ACKNOWLEDGMENTS

The longest journey begins with a single step. My personal journey has been over 40 years in the making. Several people have been influential on my path although many have no idea of their contributions to my development. Primarily, I would like to acknowledge my Father and Mother, James and Joyce Alexander who instilled in my years ago the importance of striving to be the best at what you do. You all taught me that anything is indeed possible if you believe and are willing to work hard. To my friend and Martial Arts Instructor, Soke Rob Williams, Grandmaster of the Hoshinjutsu Budo Ryu. Thank you, brother, for taking up the mantle once Glenn passed on and for keeping the system that has played such a critical part in my life alive. Much love to you. Iron Tamer Dave Whitley, my friend, and teacher. There is an irony and synchronicity in how we met and that we share the same birthday. Thank you, brother, for teaching me the art and science of the Olde Time Strongman and the mindset needed to twist horseshoes, bend spikes, and break chains. It is my hope that I will be able to inspire, encourage and empower as you have and help others achieve their dreams. Dr. Yvette Ghormley's guidance enabled me to achieve a level of academic achievement reserved for the top 3% of the world's population and earn the title Doctor. Commander Reginald (Red) Brown is one of my mentors and taught me the meaning of Servant Leadership and that to never be too proud to do a task. There are so many more to thank for all the experiences that I have had in my life that ultimately contributed to me being the person I am today.

INTRODUCTION

The book you hold in your hands is the story of a true warrior scholar. To meet Dr. Alexander in person can be an intimidating experience. He exemplifies true intensity. His drive and spirit are a testimonial of the journey he has taken to get to where he is, a top tier professional martial artist and educator. Dr. Alexander was sent to me nearly 20 years ago by my teacher, Dr. Glenn J. Morris, PhD to continue his journey through the Hoshin martial system. James was always ahead of his peers in focus and intuitive deduction of what needed to be practiced to achieve his next level of mastery. Watching him endure the challenges he has faced both personally and professionally allowed me to witness a man of honor, bravery, and endurance. In this intimate book, Dr. Alexander exposes his life as an open book, both with humility and courage to share what he has experienced, and how it gave him the fuel to drive him beyond normal limitations. I am very proud to call him my friend, student, and brother.

Though he has reached the highest attainable level in the Hoshin martial system, he approaches new lessons as a beginner. I have never seen a person as powerful and humble as Dr. Alexander. He is a living manifestation of the power of self-discipline.

Rob Williams, Soke

Grandmaster of Hoshinjutsu Budo Ryu

"We are all a product of our experiences and our environment."

Prologue

Bullying is Destructive, but you can rise from the ashes to achieve greatness. You just need to believe that it is possible….believe in the impossible. Do you believe that you have the power to overcome adversity and break out of the shackles of self-doubt that have held you back? Do you? For the majority of my life, I have contemplated this very question.

I am a 23-year Veteran of the United States Navy. Yes, I am a sailor, a Hospital Corpsman, and a Naval Officer. I have had the opportunity to visit two dozen countries and nearly every continent on the planet in service to this country. I love the United States of America; she has provided me and my family opportunities in education, training and upward mobility that would be difficult if not impossible to match anywhere else in the world. I don't mention these things to be boastful. I am no more talented or intelligent than any of you. It is my hope that after you read my story of the challenges that I have overcome to have a great life and continue improving who I am, you too will believe that the same is possible for you.

I served in the military from 1988 to 2012. After I retired from the service, I started my second career with the North Carolina Department of Public Safety, and in my current profession, I am the Chief Executive Officer of the Health Care Facility at the Women's Prison in Raleigh, NC. At the writing of this book, I would have been at Women's prison for six years. On my first day at work, my wife Renee was trying to help me decide what I was going to wear. She picked out this nice pink dress shirt for me to wear and I said *"I ain't wearing no pink shirt to a prison. It is a prison, can't let them see weakness!"* Mind you that up to this point, the only experience that I had with corrections or prisons was the Shaw Shank Redemption, Beyond Scared Straight, Cool Hand Luke, and MSNBC Lock-up. During employee orientation, my new boss, Warden Bianca Harris said *"Alexander, you have a lot of presence, and that can be frightening to your staff and to the inmates. You have to learn how to tone that down because I don't want you scaring my inmates and my staff."* When I got home from work that evening, I said to my wife, *"baby, where is that pink shirt?"*

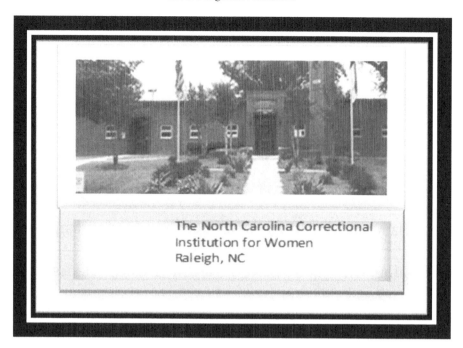

The North Carolina Correctional
Institution for Women
Raleigh, NC

What Warden Harris told me had me thinking. That is not the first time I have heard that. I have heard similar my entire professional life. *"You are so serious; you should smile more, or you are scary, you look so angry; as soon as you walk into a room your presence takes over; and you are overwhelming."* Why was I so intense? Why do I despise bullying and hate bullies in positions of power? Why did I ask my senior executives at my first staff meeting at the Prison in 2012 to help keep me in check because I know that I can be overwhelming? Why do I have checks and balances in place to protect my people from me as my position as Chief Executive Officer comes with near absolute power? Why after 40 years do I still constantly train my body, mind, and spirit? How did I finally break free of the shackles of self-loathing, self-doubt, and self-limiting beliefs and behaviors? All these aspects of myself were intentionally cultivated and over four decades in the making to serve as a subtle warning to others that I will not be a victim, nor will I victimize others. Who I am today, the man I would eventually become was a direct response to a year's long verbal bullying ordeal that occurred during my youth.

High School Graduation, June 9, 2018! Go Joselyn!

"Few things in life are as important as family."

CHAPTER 1

Age of Innocence: The Early Years

I was born November 23rd, 1967 in Oklahoma City, Ok at 11:59 pm on Thanksgiving Day to James and Joyce Alexander. In 1971, my younger brother Steve came along. Up until 1978, I had the perfect childhood. We took family trips to Dallas, TX to see the Texas Rangers and go to Six Flags, to Houston to see the Houston Astros, and go to Astro World, Oklahoma Sooner's Football games, sports, weight lifting, family gatherings over the holidays, camping trips and it goes on. Additionally, I was a straight-A student. My parents and family instilled within me, that if I am willing to work hard and apply myself, I can achieve anything such as becoming President of the United States, become an attorney, judge, or a military officer; I could also achieve things that some considered impossible.

Circa 1970's. Getting Ready for Church. From Left to right: Steve, me, and Momma

Mom and Dad worked extremely hard to provide me and Steve a great life. We wanted for nothing and always seemed to have abundance. Momma managed women's and children's clothing store and was the best at what she did. I have always been of the impression that in another time under other sets of circumstances, Momma could have been the CEO of a Fortune 500 company. She was that good. People just loved her, and she could sell to anyone.

My momma as the manager of the women's and children's clothing store "Streets".

My dad was a firefighter at Tinker Air force Base in Oklahoma. Dad has the honor of being the first black person to rise to the level of a Fire Chief at Tinker. To me, my dad was Superman. I got to see him in his prime playing softball for the fire department. Dad is also a veteran who played baseball and basketball for the United States Air Force.

Dad when he was a Fire Chief at Tinker Air Force Base in Oklahoma. Yep, that is the Space Shuttle in the background.

My dad is one of the strongest human beings that I know, and I have yet to see him ever get sick. I remember in the 70's dad's softball team played for and won the championship. I and Steve had the best time as the celebration went early into the morning at Tinker. That night seemed as if it happened yesterday; those were the days.

Little League Baseball. Those were the days.

Dad got me into baseball. He worked with me, and within the course of a season, I went from horrible player to the most improved. By the end of the next year, I was an all-star little league baseball player for a few years. He taught me the crow hop so that I could put a little extra behind my throws from the outfield. He also taught me the trick of hitting the curveball. Steve became a great baseball player at the high school and collegiate level. Dad was tireless as he

worked with both of us.

Circa 1970's. Me, Momma, Daddy, Steve and a cousin I can't remember on a beach in Texas.

I remember one year we had taken a family trip to

Dallas, TX to see the Texas Rangers and the New York

Yankees play. The traffic to get to the stadium was a virtual parking lot, and Dad had to use the bathroom. Dad got out of the car and went into a hotel to use the bathroom. When dad came out, we had moved with the traffic about a quarter of a mile down the street. I just remember seeing daddy running back to the car and finally caught us and got back in. We never made it to the game as it was sold out, so we went to Six Flags instead. Dad was fast, and I inherited my speed from him. One time I thought I could beat him running and he quickly showed me that he was still the man.......... I loved my life. There was a lot of love in the Alexander household.

October 2016: Mom and Dad's 50th Wedding Anniversary celebration.
From left to right: Steve Alexander, Joyce Alexander, James L. Alexander and me, James F. Alexander

My mom and dad had big families. I spent a great deal of time with my mom's parents, my grandparents Frank and Vinnie McClarty / Papa Mack and Momma Mack. Often my mother's brothers and sister Uncle Frank, Uncle Ronald, and Aunt Joann would babysit me and Steve. The often seemed like older siblings more than uncles and aunty as we had a lot of fun together be it at the park or just sitting around watching television. One of my fondest memories is when

Uncle Frank, Steve and I were watching *"Cooley High,"* and on the commercial breaks, we all would start wrestling and laughing. Once, the entire family took a big camping trip to Lake Texoma, TX. It was during this time that I learned about fishing, and how to fight off snakes from Pa Pa Frank. Ma Ma Vinnie was a tough old bird, and she was not one to be trifled with. Don't mess with her family or mess with her Pastor or all hell would break loose. She was the original Medea, and I often imagined that Tyler Perry modeled his character after Momma Mack.

Me and my Lady hanging out in Colorado Springs, Colorado in the Spring of 2011.

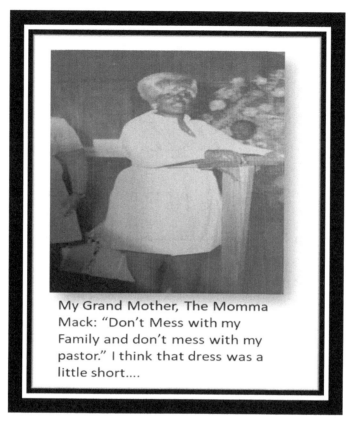

My Grand Mother, The Momma Mack: "Don't Mess with my Family and don't mess with my pastor." I think that dress was a little short....

My dad's parents, Howard and Ethel Alexander lived in rural Bristow, OK. As far as I could recall, me and Steve would spend part of every summer in Bristow. I can remember what seemed like every morning Ma Ma Ethel cooking breakfast and on the radio station, I would hear Charlie Daniels' "The Devil when down to Georgia" along with other Country and Western singers. This is where my love of country music started. In Bristow is where my dad's cousins introduced me to horseback riding and greyhound dogs. Pa Pa Howard was an imposing man. He taught me and Steve how to make bow and arrows, slingshots, and I got my first pocket knife from him. He was the individual who enlightened me on my mortality when I was five years old explaining that we all must one day die.

Summer 2011: My grandma and my Niece. From Left to right: Taylor Alexander, Ethel Alexander and me,

Oklahoma is considered part of the Bible Belt. My family was religious, and I was raised in the Baptist Church with a foundation in the Bible which meant every Sunday, and Wednesday we were at church. There were also youth programs which usually included an Easter and Christmas event. Without realizing it at the time, I got my start with public speaking in the church. Every holiday event, momma would sign me up to recite a speech or sing a solo in front of the congregation. I practiced until I was perfect and then performed flawlessly every time. Again, during this time, I felt I could do anything. After all, Santa Claus and the Easter Bunny were very real to me. Life was good, I had friends, and out of youthful ignorance, I was under the belief that life would always be this way. In my naiveté, I was under the impression that if you are nice to people, people would reciprocate and be nice in return.

Circa 1970's: This taken during a trip to Mexico. That was an interesting trip.

"Bullying is the weak person's imitation of strength."

CHAPTER 2

Innocence Lost: 6th Grade Middle School

I attended James K. Polk for Kindergarten, Quail Creek Elementary for the first and second grades, Western Village for my third and fourth-grade years, and North Highlands for the fifth grade. I attended all of these schools in Oklahoma City, OK. During this period, I was virtually a straight-A student. As long as I can recollect, I have been a prolific reader and read with comprehension at the collegiate level since I was in the fourth grade. What is strange and a mystery to me is that I have no memory of when I started learning to read or where my love of reading and books came from. Perhaps my love of reading came from comic books because I was fascinated by Superman, Batman, and other Superheroes.

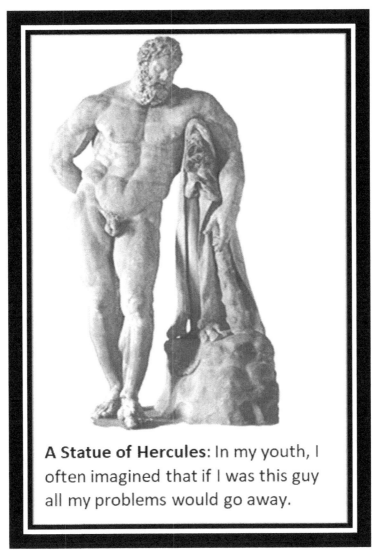

A Statue of Hercules: In my youth, I often imagined that if I was this guy all my problems would go away.

I was especially captivated by Greek Mythology especially Hercules. This was a guy who was strong and powerful, and muscular; that resonated with me. Now he had some family issues, but don't we all?

Superman was one of my Favorite Childhood Heroes. He was virtually impervious to all harm....perhaps even emotional damage.

I resonated with Batman the most because he struggled with the emotional damage of watching his parents get murdered and was haunted by those memories for years and trained relentlessly. He was also a martial artist and pretty smart.

I would also read the Bible and really enjoyed the stories. My momma put me onto Samson because I was always talking about Hercules. Momma told me Cliff Notes version of Samson's story. With excitement, I listened to Momma tell me how strong Samson was and that his strength came from God. My excitement turned to horror as she then told me that the secret of his strength was his hair and his wife cut his hair off helping his enemies blind and capture him. As a child from the traditional nuclear family, I had no examples of bad marriages. My mom and dad got along and loved each other. Imagine my confusion as I'm hearing the story of how Samson's wife did that to him. As I grew older and read the story of Samson and Delilah numerous times, I came to realize that Samson may have brought some of this on himself. He seemed to have had impulse control issues and poor decision-making habits.

When you add those variables along with super strength, a

bad outcome was bound to happen.

Samson with the Jawbone of a Donkey that he killed 1000 of his enemy with. That was a bad day for a lot of folks.

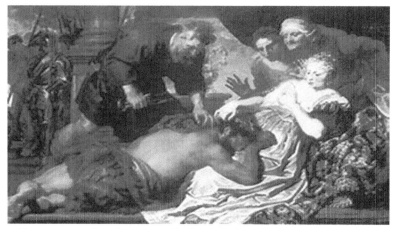

Samson being subdued by his enemies
with the help of his wife Delilah!
Imagine my horror as a young child as
my momma is telling me this story.
Who does that??

Anyway, as I stated, I was a good student during this time. I specifically remember my second-grade teacher, Ms. Mosley. She was a stern but loving, tall, slim black woman who had this afro that was immaculate. Ms. Mosley taught me how to tell time using the traditional clock and also how to multiply. Life was good. Then came the 6th grade. In the fall of 1978, I started Junior High at Hoover Middle School. Hoover was in walking distance from my home and was literally across the street from where I lived. Hoover 1978…this is where my world came crashing down, and I became acutely aware of how cruel, ugly, mean, and uncaring humans could be to one another.

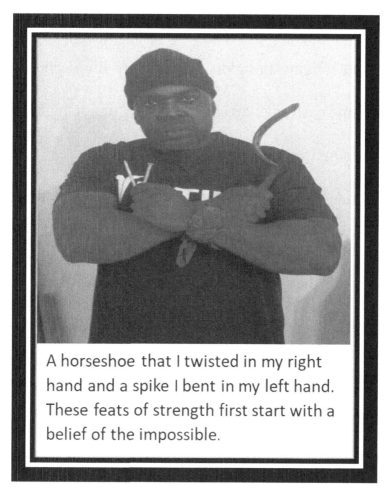

A horseshoe that I twisted in my right hand and a spike I bent in my left hand. These feats of strength first start with a belief of the impossible.

Now, I have not always been the handsome devil that I am now. No that was to come years later as I was one that peaked after my primary school years ended. In truth, as a man in my 50's, I am stronger physically, mentally, and spiritually than I have ever been at any point in my life. After all, I possess enough strength to twist horseshoes, snap baseball bats, and break chains. No wearing the letter man's jacket and reliving the glory days of my high school years for me; my best days are ahead but in junior high school, those days had yet to come.

In middle school, I found out that I was that ugly duckling that I read about. I needed braces, and I am dark skinned or as they used to call it the pejorative, Black; that is not a big thing now, especially with actors such as Wesley Snipes, Denzel Washington and many other prominent people making it cool. However, in 1978, my worth as a human being was put on trial by some of my fellow classmates, all because I was a child of the sun; I was constantly ridiculed because of it.

In the 1978-1979 school year at Hoover Middle School, I heard every black joke, such as black ass nigga, black mother fucker, and every other horrible name imaginable every single day except for two days that school year. "You must be from Africa because you are so black." "If you ever have any kids you are better off killing them because you are so ugly." If you have ever seen Eddie Murphy's The Nutty Professor, the first comic club seen, that was me every day for 9 months in school. The ringleader was a guy named Dexter Sinclair. I must tell you that Dexter Sinclair is not his real name; it is a pseudonym that I am using to protect his identity. Dexter was the class clown, popular, light-skinned, curly hair, one of those DeBarge looking brothers, or maybe that Soul Glo fellah from the movie "Coming to America." Dexter had a special name for me. He called me Juju James and the name stuck. According to my research, the Jujus are a witchdoctor sect from the Western region of Africa and since I was so black, I must be African and thus a Juju. It was all great fun for everyone, and people had a great laugh at my expense. I didn't understand why this was happening to me. Some days tears would be coming down my face, and Dexter would say, "man we just playing." I really couldn't do anything about it right? After all, they were just words. During my youth, my mom and dad had given me and Steve permission to defend ourselves….if someone put their hands on us. However, I couldn't tell my parents that people are calling me names because they were just words. The teachers were not any real help because they gave the standard "ignore them and they will go away" response. I just had to suck it up and deal with it the best way that I could.

A 2017 report of the Center of Disease Control (CDC) revealed that 21% of school-aged children experienced bullying of some fashion. As far as I know, in the 1970's verbal bullying as a concept did not exist. After all, **they were just words.** Of course, bullying in all its insidious forms is in the public psyche now due to horrendous events such homicides and suicides, but back then it was *"sticks and stones may break my bones, but words will never hurt me."* Bullshit. Whoever came up with that stupid ass slogan had no idea of the impact of words. If words can be used to inspire people to achieve greatness, words can also be used to harm individuals. Words can stab at the core of your being, cause depression, make you feel less than a human being, cause you to become a brooder, hate, question your worth as a person, become withdrawn, overreact, hesitant, etc. If words can't hurt, they can't help either, and we all know that is not true. Words can be your source of fuel and inspiration that enable you to become the first Sailor in the family, the first Naval Officer, the first Academic Doctor, and the first Chief Executive Officer who happens to bend horseshoes. You truly can overcome your hurts and accomplish greatness to be successful despite your

25

detractors. However, this version of myself was still in the future and had yet to come to fruition.

In 2017, the CDC reported that up to 21% of school aged children experienced bullying in some fashion.

I was depressed and withdrawn during this period and during the years that followed. I probably suffered from Post-Traumatic Stress Disorder (PTSD) as well. Research has revealed that children that were victimized by either physical or mental bullying often suffered from PTSD. Additionally, researchers noted that PTSD could make it difficult to concentrate, sleep and perform many of the basic tasks of daily living. Of course, back in the 1970's PTSD was mostly reserved for Vietnam War Veterans and it was normally referred to as Shell Shock. I was also physically ill a great deal; the sickly child. It would not be anything for me to be out of school for weeks on end for some illness in which I could not keep any food down and I was tired all of the time. Studies have revealed that bullying can cause depression, anxiety, and physical illness. Some days, I would feign illness, so I would not have to go to school. My focus in the 6th grade was to make it to Friday, and I would get a break from ridicule over the weekend. On Sunday's the news broadcast 60 Minutes came on CBS and in my mind that marked the end of the weekend and my anxiety would start to kick in as I prepared myself what was to come starting Monday morning as the cycle began anew.

The entire school year was a perpetual nightmare which seemed to have no end, day after day, and month after month. My teacher, Ms. Adder would often get on me about daydreaming. I wasn't necessarily daydreaming; I was imagining coming to school and being able to learn and not deal with all the craziness. My grades plummeted. This straight-A student was now a D and F student. Research has shown that students who expend energy dealing with bullying and attempting to suppress the associated painful memories have less capacity to focus on school work. To my parents, I was just not getting my school lesson, and they could not understand why. The teachers would call the house and tell my mom and dad how horribly I was doing in school, and I would get punished for it, but I never told my folks what I was experiencing; I kept this to myself. After all, they were only words. My parents tried to figure out what was going on with my grades and my mother had parent-teacher conferences with my instructors. Momma asked me one time what my problem was? I shrugged and told her that I didn't know. However, I wanted to say *"Well momma, **EVERY SINGLE DAY** a lot of my classmates pick on me. They don't put their hands on me, but they call me names constantly, all day long, tell me how ugly and black that I am. They call me African, and Juju James because those as dark as me must be from Africa. They also tell me that I should kill myself and if I have any kids, I should kill them as well because I was so black and ugly. As this is going on, the teachers sit there and let it happen; they don't attempt to intervene. When I tried to bring it up to the teachers, all they would tell me was to ignore them, and they would eventually leave me alone. I don't feel safe at school, I am sad and depressed all the time and the only time I do feel safe is when I am sick and don't have to go to school. However, since they are just words, and I have been told that words should not hurt us, I didn't feel that I could fight them without getting into trouble. So, I just sit there all day,* *every day taking it with tears in my eyes. Of course, being constantly harassed is counterproductive to getting my education because I can't focus, I am always afraid, and my feelings are constantly being hurt. I did not tell you and daddy because they were just words and I was ashamed that words had this much power over my life."* Words do indeed matter.

Thank God that the school year finally ended and somehow, I passed. It had to be a social promotion because my grades were horrible. On the last day of school, I promised myself that the seventh grade and every succeeding year would not be a repeat of the sixth grade: ***"Never again."*** I felt like I was slowly suffocating with my chest getting tighter and my life was slowly draining away. I had to break free of this tragedy and start re-claiming control of myself.

Arm shackle break during a strength performance in 2017. This can be thought of as a metaphor for freeing yourself from emotional and psychological bondage.

"If you know how to fight and look like you can bench press a Buick, people are less likely to bully you."

CHAPTER 3

Summer Break: Victim no Longer

My dad bought me my first weight set when I was around seven years old. I just remember looking in the back of the comic books, and there would be these advertisements about getting stronger and developing a muscular physique. Charles Atlas had his Dynamic Tension program that promised to turn you into Hercules in no time fast. Dad told me that it would take years to look like those guys in the back of the comic books. I would play with the weights on and off for a few years. However, I became serious about strength training and fitness after my 6th-grade year, and this dedication has remained with me throughout my life. I was determined that I would never go through what I endured ever again and if I had to fight every day to prevent it from happening, so be it.

Over the summer, I delved into my weight training, bodyweight training, and martial arts. I trained 6-8 hours every single day except for Sundays (Church). I remember daddy saying *"Boy, you can't work out all day every day, you are going to hurt yourself."* I would respond, *"Okay daddy"* and go right back to training in weightlifting, karate, boxing, and calisthenics. My mom and dad blessed me with the potential for great strength and speed and as the weeks went by and I got stronger, faster, muscular, and more confident; I started walking straighter. I also grew about 4 inches over the summer. My mom and dad also took me to the dentist to have braces put on to straighten out my teeth; the ugly duckling started his transformation into a swan. When I wasn't physically training, I would read all that I could find on combat, philosophy, spirituality, and anatomy. Momma had these female health books on the self, and I would look through these books trying not to be embarrassed hoping to find information on the human body, and the skeletal system. I needed to know where to hit a person and cause the most damage to him. I studied well and had continued my education to this day. I studied everything that I could find out about Bruce Lee and his fighting system, the way he trained and his thoughts on combat. Here was a small guy at about 5 foot, 3 inches tall, weighing about 135 pounds and he was a bad man. Now if I could become him over the summer, that would be great.

Bruce Lee from Enter the Dragon. I envisioned that I was him as I trained relentlessly over the summer after my 6th grade year.

I have dedicated my life to the study and perfection of violence praying that I will never need to use my education. There are 206 bones in the adult human body, and approximately 5 pounds of pressure per square inch can break most bones if you strike at the correct angle. Applying the appropriate amount of pressure on the carotid arteries can render a person unconscious in less than 5 seconds. A slap on the Vagus nerve can drop a person's blood pressure causing them to black out in an instant. A straight stab deep into the solar plexus can puncture the aorta and the person will be dead before they hit the ground. If you disrupt the respiratory system, the circulatory system, or the central nervous system, the fight is over. However, I have learned over the years that the greatest weapon is the one that you never have to draw. If you let me, I will walk away and wish health and prosperity. A smile and soft answer really can turn away wrath.

Brothers in arms some 30 Plus years removed from the events of my 6th grade year. Left to right: Shihan Brady Hansen, Shihan Katon Banner, Soke Rob Williams, me, Shihan Joel Artz, and Shihan Chris Robinson.

The days started to blur together as I continued training. If I ever thought about slacking off or taking a day off, I would think of Dexter and his "Juju James" comments. Finally, the summer ended, and the 7th grade was around the corner. My anxiety started to come back as the first day of school approached. *"Great...here we go again."* For a moment, I almost succumbed to total despair. However, in a fraction of a second, I made up my mind that if I had to fight every single day, I was adamant that the 7th grade would not be a repeat of the sixth grade. It didn't take long for those words to come to fruition. Thursday, of the first week of school, I was at my locker between classes, and I heard Dexter Sinclair coming down the hall talking loudly. My heart started racing, and then I heard it, "here he is, Juju James!" He came and stood beside me and said, "Hey Juju!" In a split second, the die was cast, and the decision was made. I turned fast to my left and hit him with a straight right surprising him, catching him squarely on the nose and followed that punch up with a left hook that landed solidly on the right side of his face. Dexter grabbed his face, stumbled, hit the ground and then I was on him. I kicked him in the ribs and stomped on his feet and legs, a condition known as the bloodlust had come over me as the memories of the previous year returned to me. I stomped on him repeatedly. All he could do was cover his head to prevent me from damaging his face. Finally, my old 6th-grade teacher Ms. Adder pulled me off him and took me to the Vice Principal's office.

Several things changed after that day: (1)There was no more bullying ever as I became known as the dude who could fight, (2) this solidified my love of martial arts and self-improvement and fitness, because if you know how to fight and look like you can bench press a Buick, people generally don't bother you, and (3) I got in trouble and the Vice Principle awarded me one week of in school suspension for fighting as it looked like I beat up Dexter for no reason; Dexter knew. Oh yes, Dexter knew what that ass whooping was all about. He probably suffered from PTSD after the drubbing I gave him. If this event had taken place a few years later, I could have seriously hurt this guy because I continuously trained and really started understanding combat anatomy. Luckily, I didn't have any more issues with Dexter or anyone for that matter, but the damage to my psyche from the previous year had been done, and it would take me the better of 30 years to recover. ***Now, I don't recommend*** anyone addressing bullying the way that I just articulated unless your life is in imminent danger and you have no other options. However, for a moment in time in the 7th grade, I regained some semblance of peace in my life, and at least for a brief period, I was a victim no longer.

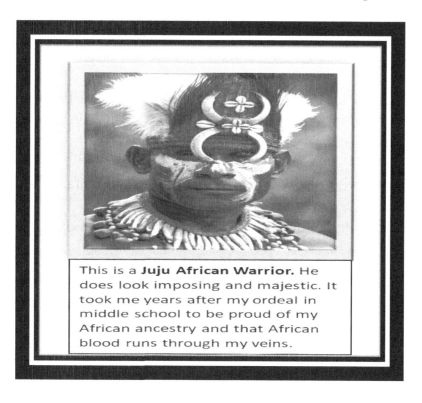

This is a **Juju African Warrior.** He does look imposing and majestic. It took me years after my ordeal in middle school to be proud of my African ancestry and that African blood runs through my veins.

"The fiercest battles that you will ever wage are those in your heart and in your mind."

CHAPTER 4

Ashes: Aftermath and the Dark Years

In the movies when a bully finally gets put in his place, the Hero rides off into the sunset with the girl, and everyone lives happily ever after. A Brady Bunch episode comes to mind in which Peter and Cindy were constantly harassed by a bully. This guy had actually punched Peter in the face giving him a black eye. After Mike and Carroll Brady tried to reason with the bully's parents to no-avail, Peter was given permission to defend he and Cindy. When the day came, and Peter fought the bully, Peter swung and struck the bully in the mouth loosening his teeth to the point that he started lisping. At the end of the show everyone made up, and the audience has the impression that all is well in the universe. If only real life was this simple.

The years following my ordeal were difficult ones that extend well into adulthood. After the thrill of beating the breaks off Dexter subsided, the demons, the painful memories of the 6th grade remained with me. It was like a virus that had I had been infected with that was dormant for a moment and reemerged at an opportune time. Those times with me could be in the classroom, lying in bed at night, a certain smell that triggered memories, etc. According to research, one of the most devious aspects of bullying or any type of abuse for that matter is that once the event or series events are over, the victim is often left with the memories, emotions, and feelings associated with the ordeal, in effect being re-victimized. This was the case with me. While nobody was victimizing me, I had become extremely self-conscious about my looks, and I was hyper-vigilant constantly on the lookout for the next person wanting to hurt me. If I noticed people whispering and looking in my directions, I automatically assumed that they were talking about and laughing at me. Well at least if they had been, it was not blatantly in my face. I constantly overreacted, and if anyone said anything that I perceived was disrespectful, as a defensive mechanism, I would be ready to fight. My grades were not much better during my 7th-grade year as I had all this emotional and mental baggage that made it nearly impossible to concentrate or focus for prolonged periods.

I became more introverted. I am an introvert by nature and being around a lot of people for prolonged periods of time drains my energy. I am happiest when I am home, either reading, working out or just hanging out with my family. When I was stationed in Long Beach, CA in the 90's, these individuals at the church I attended made it seem that being an introvert was a sin since *"Jesus wasn't an introvert."* Really? Did you ask him? Being an introvert is a sin and that's what he said? How about if I punch you in the nose? Is that a sin too? If I'm going to hell anyway for being an introvert, I may as well make it count and get my money's worth; if it sounds and feels wrong, odds are it is wrong.

As I mentioned earlier, I loved to read, and it would be nothing for me to be in my room for weeks on end reading. So, introverts give the impression that we don't like people but that is not the case at all. Solitude is how introverts recharge our emotional and mental energy. In my case, I really didn't like people or myself for that manner. My feeling was if I minimized my interaction with people, it would minimize my chances of being hurt. Of course, living my life this way has had long-range implications in my personal and professional lives. I had a difficult time processing all my emotions and expressing how I felt. Sometimes through an extreme force of will, I would suppress how I was feeling. In truth, I couldn't comprehend how I was feeling from one moment to the next. I felt like I wasn't worthy to be alive. I continued strength training and my martial arts because if anyone thought about bullying me or bothering me, I was going to try and hurt them bad. I often questioned why this had happened to me and why no one came to my assistance. Years later, as I researched this bullying phenomenon, I discovered that some people might have kept silent because they feared to become the next victim.

Negative self-talk in the second person was a constant for years. *"You ain't good enough. "Look over there; people are snickering and talking about you behind your back." "Nobody likes you; you are still ugly, they are just scared of you now."* Negative self-talk is closely related to self-esteem. Self-esteem is how individuals gauge their personal worth as a human being. Studies have shown that individuals who have been victimized by bullying often have low self-esteem. This tore at my soul for years and followed me throughout my high school years albeit not as intense as it had been in middle school. As I reflect on my past, I am certain that I suffered from some form of temporary mental illness, such as depression and anxiety. In those days, at least in my community, black people were hesitant to put much veracity in mental illness. Yes, there were mentally ill people, but that designation was reserved for institutionalized individuals. For others suffering from mental health issues, it was often thought to be from the devil and the way that you addressed that was through prayer and laying on of hands. To be fair, it has only been over the last 15 years or so that mental illness has gained the same legitimacy throughout society as physical illness; depressive disorders are just as real of a medical condition as heart disease, emphysema, or diabetes.

I never did see a therapist or mental health professional. It was through a sheer force of will, martial and spiritual practices that I would eventually conquer my negative self-talk and vanquish my demons, but that was a long time coming and once I started on this path, it would take years. However, the first step started with me deciding that I wanted to become a better human being. I eventually learned to quiet my mind and began getting my emotions under control. However, that time was still years in the future.

By the time that the 8th grade rolled around at Hoover, I was popular. I continued my martial arts practice and strength training. My body had started to really develop. I had a few friends that shared the same interest in martial arts and other topics. I was also on the track team, and the ugly duckling was becoming more of a swan with each passing month. I was a good C student, so that meant no teacher phone calls home or parent-teacher conferences. However, that voice in my head kept talking with me. *"You are an imposter. You still ain't no good because no matter how hard you work, you are still going to be really black. Yeah, you beat up Dexter, but the only reason people don't bother you anymore is because they know you can fight. Deep down, you know you are still scared, and you are still black and ugly"* Before long, the 8th grade was over, and I was about to start high school.

I started my last four years of primary school at John Marshall High school in 1981-1982 school. For the most part after my first year, I was a decent student. I never did work to my full potential during this time but every now and then glimpses of what I would eventually become would show through. I got into a couple of fights, but that had to do with testosterone stuff and emerging adulthood and not bullying. Several times people would test me only to see that I wasn't backing down, so they would back down. I still had the emotional baggage from years prior still tugging at me; I had a hard time focusing on my studies. At some point, I knew that I would need to think of life after high school. However, I was rudderless and had no clue as to what I wanted to do with my life. My family and other adults had mentioned being a Lawyer or a Journalist. Dad always reminded me that I had better get my education or I ran the risk of doing hard manual labor that did not pay well; that admonition stuck with me throughout the years.

I got my first job when I was 16 years old as a bagger at the local grocery store. By working hard and focusing, I became proficient at what I did and really enjoyed working. Having my own money was nice; I wish I had been more disciplined with my finances back then and listened to my parents. Some things you only really understand once you are out of the nest. One of my motivations for working hard was to reduce the likelihood of being ridiculed or made fun of. This was a fun job for the most part because I got to practice my hand-eye coordination as I bagged the groceries; practicing my martial art skills without realizing it. The managers liked me as well as the cashiers and my colleagues. However, there was that familiar voice in my ear whispering: *"They are only pretending to care about you because you work hard. Once you are no longer of any use to them they will turn on you, you will see."* Consistently thinking this way and feeling that the other shoe would drop has been a detriment to my life. My ability to trust others and to be open with those closest to me was non-existent. I wasn't opened with my parents most of the time and kept to myself. I did learn to start putting on a stoic expression so if something bothered me; it would be difficult to tell by reading my facial expressions. It was during this time where my body language, physique, and facial expressions started working together to put out a vibe that served as a warning:

"Screw with me at your peril." This was a defense mechanism. The issue with this was that I warned off would be friends along with any potential tormentors. I truly felt like a hermit at times as I spent increasingly more time alone. If I got into trouble, my parent would have to find a different way to punish me because being grounded and restricted to my room was right up my alley because I had my books. So, mom and dad would attempt to take my books from me. However, there were too many places to conceal my items for them to find everything.

I graduated from John Marshall in 1986, and that was that. I had been accepted in the what was then known as Central State University (University of Central Oklahoma) located in Edmond Oklahoma. My mom and dad paid for my tuition, and I attempted to take 12 hours while also working at the same grocery store that I started at when I had turned 16. I still had no idea of what I wanted to do for a living and first majored in Business Management, and then I change my major to Sociology or Criminal Justice. I still did not have any focus because I was still fighting my personal demons.

Graduation Day, May 1986 with Momma and Daddy

I met a guy at my place of employment who was a competitive bodybuilder. He took me under his wing, and I started to get serious about body building going five days per week to a place known as "The Body Shop." This was where the big boys trained, and I got to learn the secrets of getting big and strong. Since they knew that I was a fighter, these guys accepted me into the fold. I really started putting on muscle, and people really looked at me differently, and it wasn't necessarily fear, it was more of admiration. That voice in my head wasn't as loud and started to become quiet. The ugly duckling was physically gone, and the swan was born; I still had emotional issues to deal with. However, this did come at a cost to my grades, and eventually, I would be placed on academic probation. To compound the problem, I was a soon to be father; the girl I was dating became pregnant with my son. I had some serious decisions to make. I was raised to take responsibility for my actions, and I now had responsibility and would soon to be a father. Without many viable options, I looked at the military as a way out, and 30 years later, this ended up being one of the best decisions in my life.

"We never fully get over past hurts. However, we can learn to rise above our pain to live meaningful lives."

CHAPTER 5

Rising from the Ashes: Rebirth

I enlisted in the United States Navy November 15, 1988 and went active April 18, 1989. The military is an excellent choice for the individual who needs direction and is trying to find their way in life, and that was me. I would venture to guess that most of us did not think of this as a career choice, but only as a shortstop along to something else. Much to my surprise, once I completed schooling, the Navy felt like a regular job with the exception that we wore uniforms. I liked wearing the uniform as it was the symbol of a brotherhood that represented the most powerful military the world has ever seen. I loved my time in the service as it helped to shape me into the person I am today.

My recruiter was a Boatswain's Mate First Class (E6) by the name of Phillip Thomas. Phil was a strait shooter. There have been a lot of stories about unscrupulous recruiters over the years promising everything just to get a person to sign on that dotted line. I remember walking into the recruiting station on May Avenue in Oklahoma City, OK and there was Phil. We talked a little bit, and then he gave me a practice Armed Services Vocational Aptitude Battery (ASVAB) test. Your score on ASVAB tests determines what enlisted occupations you are qualified for. I scored high on that test, so Phil set me up with the actual test.

Once I took the actual ASVAB, I scored fairly high, and the Career Advisor set me down to talk to about occupational options. One of the choices that I had was as a Hospital Corpsman. I wasn't entirely sure of what all a Corpsman was responsible for, but I knew field medicine was in the description. Hospital Corpsman it was; that decision at that moment is why 30 years later, I am working in the industry that I love so much. In actuality, medical profession chose me as much as I chose it. Being that I had at least 38 hours of college credit, I was awarded the rank of E-3 (seaman) while in basic training. Phil congratulated me on scoring so well on the ASVAB and on my career choice. I think about Phil often and wonder where he is. I wonder if he knows that he raised two Naval Officers (me and big Steve). The voice was silent. The emotional damaged remained as it was deeply ingrained, but at least the negative self-talk had vanished for the time being.

April 18th, 1989, I left the only home that I had ever known to head to Basic Training at Recruit Training Center, Great Lakes, Illinois. Although it was in the spring, it was a chilly morning in Oklahoma. I remember me, my Mom, Dad and Steve crying as I left. There were several other recruits leaving out that day with me to begin their lives as sailors as well. We flew out of Will Rogers Airport and at some time around 10:00 PM we landed in Chicago O'Hare International Airport. One thing that Phil continuously stated was that the entire boot camp experience was a head game and since I was as muscular as I was, the Company Commanders would probably pick on me. Ha! He did not lie about that. Let the games commence.

The Navy equivalent to a Drill Sergeant is a Company Commander. You could always recognize them by the red cord they wore on their left shoulder. Those first few days of boot camp were the personification of chaos. Some guys were crying wanting to go home. Others were treating boot camp like it was a big joke. I was just sitting back observing and wondering what the hell I had gotten myself into. My first night there, we got a total of 15 minutes of sleep. I was in Company 182, and we had two Black Company Commanders who were Gunners Mates. They were First Class Petty Officers (E-6) by the names of Petty Officer Henry, and Petty Officer Crawford. These guys were pretty big fellas. Petty Officer Henry reminded me of Tone Loc. He had these dark sunglasses on. Petty Officer Henry and Petty Officer Crawford were laying down the law to us would be sailors.

Company Commanders have the most difficult job in the Navy. These committed individuals are charged with transforming a group of civilians from individuals into a company of sailors in the span of two months. They spend a great deal of time with their companies during the first month after which we began operating more independently. Back in those days, they could say just about anything to us in any manner. I remember Phil telling me, listen to the instruction, not the way that it comes at you. Our Company Commanders never yelled. They had an almost comical way of disciplining us. Mashing in boot camp was physical training used as a means of disciplining the company for any infraction. During one of these evolutions, I vividly remember Petty Officer Crawford stating: *"I want you all to know something, I'm abusing you mother fuckers and I don't care. You can go tell on me, and all they are going to do is send me back out to sea. I like going to see because I like collecting the sea pay."* Years later, I still laugh about this.

Me when I was in the first or second grade and when I was in Basic Training.

Basic training had its pecking order, and it was entertaining watching people jockey for position. I sat back and did not speak much with anyone; I just watched and continued to wonder what in the world I had gotten myself into. About eight days into this experience, Petty Officer Crawford walked up to me and made a statement so profound that it set me on a course that would forever change the trajectory of my life. Crawford said: *"Alexander, everyone one of these guys in here is scared of you and you ain't said shit to any of them; you are in charge.*" I had no idea what that meant or the implications of my new position, but here I was responsible for nearly 90 other guys as the Recruit Chief Petty Officer of Company 182. This was the beginning of my foray into leadership that has spanned virtually my entire adult life. These Company Commanders saw something in me that I had not yet seen in myself. If truth be known, my hope was to fly under the radar and not get noticed. It was safer that way and less chance of being ridiculed. As fate had it though, this was not to be.

This leadership education was trial by fire and knowledge by a firehose. I was responsible for getting the company prepared for school, meal time, inspections, drill, and physical training. I learned about delegation of responsibilities as I had a staff that assisted me in running the company. Man, there were a lot of growing pains, and I stayed in the hot seat for one reason or another as we slowly but surely made the transformation from civilians in training to sailors. I had a few guys try me when the Company Commanders were not around. This huge guy by the name of Berryhill challenged me to arm wrestling. Berryhill outweighed me by at least 60 pounds and was about 5 inches taller than me; I arm wrestled him to a standstill. Another instance, one of the guys came, and bear hugged me in the front goofing around, and I threw 20 punches or so in the span of about six seconds lightly tagging him on the face and nose. Everyone's mouth hit the ground as they stood just shaking their heads. My confidence increased a little more, and I remembered my self-admonition from middle school: *"If you know how to fight and look like you can bench press a Buick, people generally will not bother you."*

As we were all in close quarters, it was easy to get sick with colds and other communicable diseases. I got sick during this time with some upper respiratory infection that lasted the nearly two months that I was in boot camp. But my pride and dedication to my team would not allow me to quit. I remember our last graded physical fitness evolution which included a little over a two-mile formation run and I was sick, feverish, and weak and had lost about 20 pounds in 6 weeks. About a 1/2 mile into the run, I was in trouble, my legs felt like rubber, I couldn't control my breathing and started to hyperventilate, and the voice that had been quiet for so long returned and started taunting me, telling me that I was no good and that I was going to let my company down, be a disappointment to my family, not graduate on time, and that I was never going to amount to anything. It was here that I finally killed **THAT** voice that had haunted me for years and said NO! I had come too far to fail. I shut all mental processes off in my head (*I didn't know I could do that, until that moment*) and just concentrated on breathing and continuing to move. I had resigned that I would die before ever quitting and letting my squad down. At one point in the run, my Assistant Recruit Chief said: *"Alexander, slow down."* I was at the head of the formation leading the group and was starting to pull away. Finally, the run was over, we all passed, and from that moment forward, all the Company Commanders viewed us a bit differently, almost as colleagues or shipmates. Our boot camp graduation which is known as the Pass in Review was a few short days away. There would be other voices in the form of self-doubt, first person negative self-talk, and the imposter syndrome that would surface from time to time, but I finally slew that specific tormentor for good. I have come to realize that working on your self-esteem and confidence is a lifelong pursuit. If I don't continuously strive to improve I fear that the voice may return.

Family Day is the day before the Pass in Review in which we will parade in front of the reviewing party. This day is typically Thursday evening with the Pass in Review being Friday Morning. This was the first time my family has seen me in two months. I remember marching the squad into the drill hall where our family members were waiting. My family hardly recognized because of the weight that I had lost, and they could tell that I was sick. Petty Officer Crawford had told my parents how I was placed in charge of the company: *"We told Alexander that all of the guys in here were scared of him and he had not said anything to anybody."* Petty Officer Crawford cleaned the statement up for my parents.

Friday Morning was the Pass in Review. We staged in the practice drill hall before beginning our march to the official drill hall where hundreds of visitors, guest and family members were waiting for us to arrive. I remember marching down towards the official drill hall as we passed a company that just arrived to basic training. I saluted that group's company commander and he returned my salute telling his company: *"That can be you in eight weeks men. There will be hundreds of people there to watch them at the Pass in Review."* Once we arrived at the drill hall, we stood there for what seemed like hours. During rehearsal we were advised to not lock our legs because some of us may pass out due to decreased blood circulation; several individuals passed out in the graduation rehearsal, and those same individuals passed out at the actual event. The medical crew was present to tend to them both times. Before long, the Commanding Officer of the Recruit Training Command gave his remarks and told us that we earned the right to be called sailors as we prepared to march around the drill hall and present ourselves before the reviewing stand and official party: *"Color Company and companies in succession, forward march!"* The Color Company was the company with the highest score from our graded evolutions. The band started playing *"Anchors Aweigh."* Each of the company Recruit Chief Petty Officers had to be queued when to start marching their respective companies, and from the point forward, we guided our men around the drill hall. Finally, Company 182's time had come, and I was given the signal. I commanded: *"Company forward march!"* We all stepped off on our left foot as I was to the left center of my company. As we marched down one length of the drill hall, time appeared to slow down. A slight smile came across my face, as I was in the zone, we were in the zone; out of my peripheral vision, I noticed how well my guys moved. Even now, 30 years later (**at the writing of this book**), chills come over me when I think about that day. The sounds, smells, and feelings became a permanent part of me. My family was there somewhere watching as I was about to call my first movement: *"By the left flank march!"* This movement put me from the left center of the company to the front center of my company as all 90 of us transitioned as a single unit from marching to flanking left to marching in one fluid motion. After the pass in review was over, I was told by several people including Petty Officer Crawford, that the first movement was a thing of beauty. As my company approached the reviewing stand, we rendered the salute on my command: *"Company eyes right!"* Before I knew it, the ceremony was completed, and we got to go on liberty with our families. Mom and dad got me some medication that helped me get better. Approximately one week later, we were done with boot camp, and I was onto my next challenge. There was one thing that Petty Officer Crawford told the group right before we left basic training that stuck with me: *"From this day forward, you will never initiate a salute with another enlisted person."* Up to that point, we saluted all Commissioned Officers and Company Commanders. In truth, when we first got to basic training, we were saluting everyone including the maintenance personnel. One time when me and one of my buddies were on liberty in downtown Chicago, we saluted these two airline pilots thinking they were military officers. Hey, when in doubt salute! Interestingly enough, it would be approximately 11 years later when I received my first salute from an enlisted person when I became a commissioned officer.

Boot Camp was a formative part of my young adulthood. This was the beginning of my leadership journey and path to self-discovery. Unfortunately, I don't remember the names of any of the guys that I spent so much time with. Because of my past experiences with bullying, it was difficult to trust people which made it challenging to build and sustain meaningful relationships. This is part of my challenge, and it will remain with me for the rest of my days.

After boot camp, it was off to Hospital Corpsman School at Naval Training Command which was across the street from Naval Recruit Training Command. The Hospital Corp has a great history and heritage of sacrifice, honor, and tradition. Hospital Corpsmen have served at the forefront of war and conflict alongside the Marines, at sea or in military treatment facilities. Hospital Corps School or Corps School was 15 weeks long, and we learned the basics of field medicine to include emergency treatment. Because of my position in boot camp, as the Recruit Chief, and my previous college experience, I was placed in charge of the class. We had military and academic advisors who guided us through the class. Corps School was a lot like living on a college campus. Gone were the open bay barracks and they were replaced with four-person dorm rooms. I got to grow as a leader as I was still finding my way; my love for healthcare and helping people started here. Fifteen weeks flew by at breakneck speed, and in October of 1989, I was off to Pharmacy Technician School at the Naval School of Health Sciences, Portsmouth Detachment in Portsmouth Virginia for 26 weeks of special training in pharmaceuticals, pharmacology. This school wasn't my choice but came due to needs of the Navy. I am glad that I had this opportunity.

Navy Pharmacy Technicians were trained differently than what you may think of as a CVS or rite aid pharmacy technician. Our school schedule was eight hours per day, five days per week, for six months along with our clinical rotations. We learned how to operate independently of a pharmacist in the field as well as how to support the pharmacist when working inside of military treatment facilities. We intimately learned about the therapeutic and toxic values of approximately 2000 different medications; we were well trained. I was not in much of an official leadership position here, and that was okay with me. It is okay to be a follower at times. I have come to realize that to be a good leader, you must also be a good follower. In pharmacy technician school, I continued my strength training as my physique really started changing and becoming more muscular. Because I often brooded, I looked like a bruiser. However, I was pretty popular as I worked hard to be a likable person. The last thing that I ever wanted was to become that which I despised. I would never become a bully as I had first-hand knowledge of how destructive bullying is. Over the years, I would become one who would stand up for those who didn't feel that they had a voice. At my present job, my motto has become I despise bullying, and I hate bullies in positions of authority. Being the boss has its advantages, as I fight for those who can't fight for themselves. I encourage and empower people to fight their own battles until they can't fight anymore; this is where I intervene. Pharmacy

Technician school had its difficulties, but I graduated with a 93% average and dedicated myself to mastering my craft and profession; not bad Alexander. Once I graduated in the spring of 1990, I received my orders to Naval Hospital Long Beach, CA.

Each success that I had, buried my middle school experiences a little deeper. However, I still had not truly recovered from that experience as from time to time the memories of this ordeal would trigger anger, sadness, and depression if only for a moment before I pushed the memories back into a compartment deep in my subconscious mind. As I reflected, I realized that often, I was successful in my adult life **To Spite** my detractors instead of being successful **In Spite** of my past. In 1993 while I was stationed in Long Beach, CA, I found a book at B. Dalton Books titled "Path Notes of an American Ninja Master" by Glenn J. Morris. Glenn who would later become a friend and teacher was the founder of a martial system called Hoshinjutsu. Glenn had several black belts in other martial arts systems and was also a Master Ninjutsu practitioner under Grandmaster Masaaki Hatsumi. Hoshinjutsu would eventually become my primary martial art. Glenn spent time in the Army and interestingly enough he was a medic. His book was classified as a martial art psychology manual. Other than the Bible, this guide has had more influence on my life than any other manual. I had practiced the martial arts for years and had two phenomenal teachers while stationed in Long Beach; the martial path had become a way of life for me. When I found Path Notes, I was looking for more along the spiritual path. Something that would help me find inner peace and finally kill the remaining demons of my middle school years. My ordeal in the 6th grade seemed like a lifetime ago. I was not the same person, but I still carried the burdens and scars of that time. There were several Taoist Chi Kung exercises in Path Notes that dealt with spirituality, posture, quieting my mind, contemplation and breathing that eventually helped me find peace.

Meditation taught me how to quiet my mind so that I could start healing from my trauma.

However, I had to confront and not run from that which haunted me for years and finally deal with how I allowed those demons to have so much power over my life before I finally achieved peace. It was during this time that I came to realize that we never fully heal from our past hurts, but we can learn to live above the pain and have joyful lives. Peace is a journey, and I have to constantly work to maintain it. Glenn died in 2006 while I was deployed with the 22nd Marine Expeditionary Unit, to Iraq. He passed suddenly into the void, and the mantle of his system passed on to my teacher and close friend, Rob Williams. Hoshin has remained my primary martial system for nearly 30 years. In actuality, once you reach the top of the mountain, all systems are similar, and it becomes a matter of personal expression.

The Late Dr. Glenn J. Morris, Founder and Grandmaster of the Hoshinjutsu Budo Ryu

There will always be detractors in life. I remained in Long Beach until 1995 when I received orders to the USS Abraham Lincoln CVN-72 which is a Nuclear-Powered Aircraft Carrier. The Lincoln is approximately 3.5 football fields long, weighs 100,000 tons and can hold in excess of 4,000 individuals.

The USS Abraham Lincoln, CVN-72 which is an Aircraft Carrier. With the capacity to hold up to 5,000 people, this is the equivalent to a small city.

I made some good friends on the Lincoln that thanks to social media, I am in contact with till this day. On the USS Abraham Lincoln, I had a detractor by the name of Senior Chief Hospital Corpsman Jergunson (pseudonym). It wasn't just me; it was all of the black enlisted people in the medical department. Jergunson wore the khaki uniform of the senior enlisted person, but it should have been a white sheet, hood and burning cross. I called him out for being a good ole boy, and as much as he may have tried to prevent it, I still made E-6 because I was that good. However, he did some things to probably prevent me from making Chief (E-7) my first and only time I would be up for that promotion, but guess what mother fucker, I got commissioned a few months later and left the enlisted ranks behind. You stayed clear of me, and our paths never met again. You, my friend, were the definition of a bully in a position of power and are the reason that I despise people such as you. I was the baddest man in the medical department and in a crew of up to 5,000; I had few equals on the Lincoln. The Marines trained with me in unarmed combat. If I had not had anything to lose, I would have beaten you within an inch of your life, permanently disfiguring you, and took my time in the Brig. By this time, I had years of combat and strength training behind me and could break whatever I hit. In spite of your efforts you, racist coward, and to spite you, less than three years later in 2001, I was a Naval Officer, and you would have saluted me. If you would have had an issue with that, we could take off the collar devices and discussed it. Again, bullies are weak people masquerading as strong people. As a leader, if the people around you are not stronger because of you, you are the problem. I read a quote from the Dali Lama once where he stated that if you can't help a person, at the very least do nothing to harm them. Bullies in leadership positions are weak people who cause more harm than good to individuals and organizations. Ask me why I despise bullies in positions of authority, and I go back to my time on the USS Abraham Lincoln. Never be that person. I hate bullies.

USS Abraham Lincoln heading for Somalia during a crisis. Her top speed is classified but she is going fast enough to leave a three mile wake.

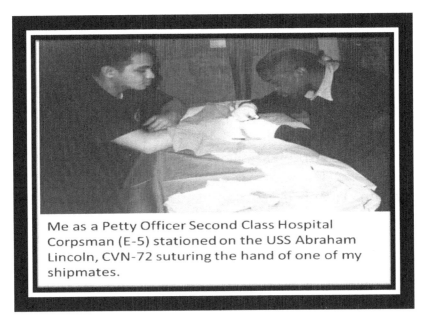

Me as a Petty Officer Second Class Hospital Corpsman (E-5) stationed on the USS Abraham Lincoln, CVN-72 suturing the hand of one of my shipmates.

I had worked hard in the Navy to better myself and help those around me. One of the things that I truly miss in the Navy that you don't find in many other organizations is that sense of camaraderie. In the military, teamwork is a matter of life and death, and we treated that as such. One of my goals and dreams since joining the Navy was to ultimately become a commissioned officer. I knew that for that to become a reality to me, I had to complete the college education that I had begun after high school. Now I had direction, drive, and ambition. In 1999 as the Leading Petty Officer of the Pharmacy at Naval Hospital Bremerton, in Charge of 26 other technicians while supporting our pharmacist in pharmacy operations, I was selected, Sailor of the Quarter and eventually the Sailor of the Year, and in August of 2000, I completed my Undergraduate Degree with Bachelor of Science in Healthcare Administration. One-time dad had asked me what my grades looked like, and I told him A's and B's. He said, *"Damn boy, you are busier now than you were when you lived at home."* I said, *"Yeah daddy, but now I'm paying for it."* We laughed at that one. I ended up graduating with a 3.33 GPA which was good for me.

In September 2000, I thought I had a good shot at making Chief, but that was not my reality. I felt that I had let everyone down and doubt had set in as to what my future was going to be. I was dejected and felt like an imposter; I was the President of the First-Class Petty Officer Association, a mentor to junior sailors, who was not good enough to make Chief Petty Officer. However, our Executive Officer, Captain Dan Snyder reminded me of what my ultimate goal was and stated: *"You will not even remember this day when your commissioning comes."* In October of 2000, I found out that I had been selected for commissioning as a Naval Officer and in March of 2001, I was commissioned as an Ensign into the Medical Service Corps as a Healthcare Administrator and a first generation Military Officer. Becoming a Naval Officer is where my healthcare executive career began. I know I know, I have heard all of the jokes. **Medical Service Corps / MSC**, **M**issed **S**election for **C**hief. There is nothing like some good natured ribbing among colleagues which is the culture of the military. I actually laugh at that joke every month on my way to the bank. One day after I received my commission, I had to remind this Master Chief Petty Officer **(E-9)** who was an asshole, and trying to talk shit to me, the new lowly O-1, that the senior most enlisted person in the Navy who is the Master Chief Petty Officer of the Navy **(E-10)** calls the junior most officer **(O-1) Sir.** He had this look of shock on his face and got all tongue tied as he tried for a snappy come back. I gave him a smirk turned my back and walked away leaving him and my enlisted life behind. Don't get it twisted little man. If we ain't cool, we don't joke around because it is coming from a place of malicious intent. That is how misunderstandings and bullying occur and I don't do bullying. Continued success in my endeavors despite my setbacks bred confidence, and I discovered that confidence is the antithesis to bullying. Eventually, I would completely defeat the self-limiting beliefs and actions that were part of my life for so many years. I had come a very long way since middle school, and although I was still a work in progress, I had finally figured out the way ahead.

Ensign James F. Alexander, Medical Service Corps, USN

My life as an enlisted sailor was over, and my life as an officer began; Captain Snyder was right. Not making Chief was an afterthought as I contemplated what my new life would entail. Yes, the military is indeed a great choice for the right individual.

The Golden 13: For the African American Naval Officer, our origins began in 1944 with these 13 Gentlemen who were commissioned as the first black U.S. Naval Officers. Always remember where you came from.

After my commissioning ceremony, I reflected on the importance of always remembering the individuals who paved the way for me to have the freedoms that I now enjoy. My parents, grandparents, great-grandparents, and ancestors going back countless generations sacrificed throughout the years so that I could succeed. If it were not for the sacrifices of these individuals, the success and freedom that I now enjoy would not have been possible. Once while I was on a training exercise at Little Creek, VA these older retired black veterans walked up to me and said that they were proud of me. During their time in the service, they did not *"see many black Officers."* I thanked them for their sacrifice, and for paving the way for me and those like me. Indeed, I stand on the shoulders of giants.

General Colin Luther Powell. Former Chairman of the Joint Chiefs of staff and former Secretary of State. By his own admission, he wandered aimlessly until the Army found him. The rest is history.

Me and Big Steve at his commissioning ceremony in 2007. Mom and Dad did okay. They raised two Naval Officers.

"Remaining bitter is the equivalent of drinking poison and hoping the other person gets sick."

CHAPTER 6

Rising from the Ashes: Reborn

An Officer who was prior enlisted is known as a Mustang and to the enlisted community, as long as this individual does not forget their roots, they have instant credibility because they (we) understand the issues of the enlisted folks because this is where we started. This person can also serve as a beacon and example of what hard work, preparedness and a bit of luck can achieve.

Me as a Naval Officer, LT (O3-E)

My career as a Naval Officer spanned March 2001 through April 2012 and during this time, I met many great people. The individual who has been a mentor for me from March 2001 to the current time was a humble but strong leader by the name of Reginald (Redd) Brown. I met Redd in May of 2001 when I was stationed at Halyburton Naval Hospital at Marine Corps Air Station, Cherry Point, NC. Redd was a Lieutenant in the Navy at that time and similar to me, he was a Mustang. Me being the lowly Ensign had found a role model that I could emulate. Redd was a God-Fearing man who reinforced the concept of servant leadership with me. Redd and I came from working-class families, so the idea of being too good for any task did not compute with us. Redd was smart, judicious, and I learned a great deal from him. I will never forget this one thing that he said to me: *"J, I will gladly make coffee for the Commanding Officer every single morning as long as it is adequately reflected in my fitness report. As long as what I am asked to do does not violate the law, or violate my ethics or morals, I don't have a problem with it."*

Marine Corps Air Station Cherry Point, NC. Those jets you hear flying overhead are the sounds of freedom.

CDR Reginald (Redd) Brown, USN. This is the first mentor I had as a Naval Officer.

Some of our colleagues felt that since they had advanced degrees, some tasks were beneath them and only enlisted people should perform those jobs. Hell, in the Naval Medical Department, plenty of people have a college education. Some Enlisted people have multiple degrees including their doctorates. You can't get too full of yourself. There is always somebody smarter, and better than you at something. Being an officer does not make you better than an enlisted person, only different.

In May of 2003, I transferred to Camp Lejeune in Jacksonville, NC to begin my tour with the Marines at 2nd Medical Battalion first as the Battalion Adjutant and then as the S1 (Personnel Officer). My Commanding Officer was then Commander, Ben Feril. I liked Commander Feril. He was a hardass, but he was fair, smart, and always stressed the importance of being competent and cared about his people. He sent me to a six-week battalion adjutant's school and also Expeditionary Warfare School. He wanted his officers to be equally as capable as our marine counterparts. Interesting that at my current position within the prison system, I often find myself asking *"how would Commander Feril respond in this situation."*

Captain Ben Feril, Medical Service Corps, USN. Great, Great Officer. I learned a great deal from him that I am applying as the CEO of my Healthcare Operation.

In November 2004, I transferred from 2nd Medical Battalion to the 22nd MEU (SOC) as the Medical Planner and would remain there until I transferred in August of 2006. The MEU is the tip of the spear as far as combat units are concerned. The best and smartest are part of this unit, and I was with them and a part of them. The Commanding Officer was a Marine by the name of Colonel Kenneth F. McKenzie. Because of his love of Auburn Football, he had the call sign of Line Backer One. My call sign was Linebacker Medical. Colonel McKenzie was sharp, had a trap memory and did not tolerate stupidity. He taught me how to tell the difference between the sound of an improvised explosive device (IED) exploding and a Mortar round impacting; the IED has a rolling sound following the detonation. Part of my leadership style is modeled after what I learned observing him. September 2005 shortly before deploying to the Iraq War, I completed the requirements for my Graduate Degree, MBA with a final GPA of 3.59. I had come a long way indeed and began to understand that continuing to relive the hurts of the past serves no beneficial purpose and often impeded my growth as a human being. As I reflect, I realize that I spent so many years being angry, hurt, and inhibited that I didn't have peace, happiness or enjoy the successes that I had achieved; so many years wasted living this way.

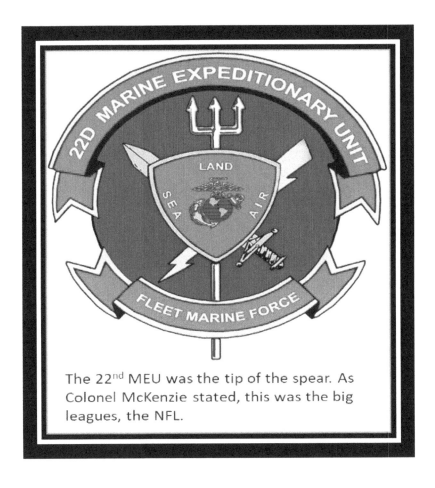

The 22nd MEU was the tip of the spear. As Colonel McKenzie stated, this was the big leagues, the NFL.

I enjoyed my time with 22nd MEU. The Marines accepted me as one of their own, and I made some friends during this time as we trained for war and eventually deployed to Iraq in support of Operation Iraqi Freedom in 2005-2006.

Lieutenant General Kenneth Frank McKenzie Jr. USMC was my Commanding Officer during my time with the 22nd MEU (SOC) 2004-2006.

One of the last things Colonel Frank McKenzie said to me as we disbanded at the end of our combat operations: *"You were a good Medical Planner Doc and calm under pressure."*

Pressure meant chaos reigned, mortars were incoming, and improvised explosive devices (IEDs) going off. I resisted the urge to run screaming in terror and focused on getting my job done. I indeed learned that courage is not the absence of fear because I was plenty afraid. Courage is the ability to continue despite your worries; damn, I was actually in the middle of a war zone. As I stated earlier as I was reliving my boot camp experience, I would die before I ever quit and fail those depending on me.

I concluded my tour with the 22nd MEU in August of 2006 to transfer to Naval Hospital Camp Lejeune, NC. From 2006 to the end of my career in 2012, time appeared to accelerate. I had family challenges that eventually led to me divorcing my first wife in 2007; sometimes outer peace in the form of removing harmful influences in your life becomes a perquisite for obtaining inner peace. I was continuing to practice my strength training, martial arts, and spiritual disciplines in my relentless pursuit of inner peace. Once you obtain inner peace,

maintaining outer peace becomes possible.

November 2005, in route to Iraq with the 22nd MEU (SOC).

Navy Ball 2007 at Camp Lejeune, NC with my second oldest child, Jazmine Alexander. Of my three biological children, we are the most alike.

It was between 2007 and 2016 that I finally subdued the remaining demons from middle school forever. It was a process of physical exercises, affirmation, success in my career, contemplation, meditation, and other steps that I will describe in the second part of this book. From March to

December of 2008, I deployed again, but this time to South America, and the Caribbean for humanitarian reasons as the Medical Operations Officer for Mission Continuing Promise.

Me and the fellas. A great bunch of guys right here.

In 2009, I transferred to United States Transportation Command (USTRANSCOM) at Scott Air Force Base, IL in what would be the final duty station of my career. When I came into the military, I always had thought that eventually, I would get out and I should always be preparing for that day. I have seen the look of despair on people's faces as they realized that they were not ready to get out of the military, but circumstances were forcing them out anyway. The Navy gave me so many opportunities. I had two college degrees at this time. I had at one point been a nationally certified Emergency Medical Technician, (EMT), I was also a nationally certified Pharmacy Technician (CPHT). Additionally, I was FEMA trained, a public speaker, a facilitator, a trained Naval Legal Officer, an Antiterrorism Officer, and I had obtained my Executive Medicine Qualification which attested that I had enough training and experience to be the CEO of a military treatment facility. Above all of this, I had the leadership experience that I honed over the years in diverse environments that no amount of formal education could ever compare with. I had been in a leadership position while at military treatment facilities, on naval warships, on the ground in Iraq, and in the underserved areas of South American and the Caribbean.

During my time in the military, a Naval Officer automatically fully qualified from O1 to O3. After O3 every promotion will come as a result of the board. I was up for O4 in 2010, and while I thought I had a good shot at making it, it wasn't to be as I got passed over. That was devastating as I tried to recover and hopefully make it in 2011although that would be a long shot as I was now above zone. I had a lot of excellent support from my supervisors and Redd Brown. I continued working hard in 2011 although I had a feeling that I was on borrowed time. I won the St Louis Navy League award and a few other honors that year. In May of 2011, at a Department of Health and Human Service conference, held in Fort Worth, TX at the Gaylord Hotel, I gave the presentation of my life in front of approximately 200 individuals. I had the pleasure of taking my daughter, Joselyn Alexander with me. If nothing else, I would go out with a bang. The Navy did me right with all of the opportunities, education, and experiences.

Joselyn F. Alexander: My Ride or die partner who has been by my side when the entire world seemed to be against me.

For an officer, under most circumstances, if you get passed over twice, you have to get out of the Navy. In 2011, I was passed over again, and that was the death knell for my military career. Again, I was devastated. I started hearing from people that I had not heard from in years offering their condolences. Always be mindful of those who only come around during times of trials, but you never hear from them at any other point in your life; it is false concern that they exhibit

(*I have not heard a peep out of these individuals since I have been retired*).

I reflected on the words that Brigadier General Ron Coleman had spoken to a group of us in 2003 when I was stationed at Camp Lejeune. He said: *"The Corps will break your heart because one day she is going to tell you that she doesn't need you anymore. Hopefully, you have put energy into those things that matter such as family. Make the Marine Corps your career and your family your life."* Although I was a sailor, I carried the admonishment of those words for the remainder of my career and carried them to this day. In truth, after the shock wore off of not being selected, I realized that I was tired. Struggles in my family life that had spanned my entire officer career had worn on me. Three deployments in a little fewer than four years had come at great personal sacrifice to my kids and they had suffered enough; I had a sole custody of a minor daughter that needed me. Mentally, I did not have the energy to continue, and it was time to move on. I have seen people who put everything into their careers sacrificing family only to find out that once the career or job was gone, so was the neglected family. I read a quote from General Colin Powell in which he stated that we cannot be so caught up in a position that once that position goes away, we fall to pieces (paraphrased). I was actually relieved to be moving on once my emotions settled. I processed out of the military and made certain my affairs were in order for my post military life. My colleagues at USTRANSCOM gave me a nice retirement party. My two favorite ladies (Renee and Joselyn) were there with me. I thanked everyone for all of their support during my time there and thanked my daughter for always being my constant over the years. I said my good byes and that was the last time I seen them.

In January of 2012, I left my last duty station at Scott Air Force Base by automobile with my new wife Renee, and my daughter Joselyn, to head to Raleigh, NC to begin the next phase of my life. With UTRANSCOM, Scott Air Force Base, and my military life in the rearview mirror; I never looked back physically, mentally, or emotionally. That phase of my life was over, and the next phase had begun. One great thing about this scenario was that I got to retire from the Navy after 23 years of service with a full pension as a Naval Officer and as a young man. Now I needed to figure out what I wanted to do for the rest of my life; I wouldn't have to wait long.

November 25, 2011, I married my best friend Lora Renee Alexander. My son James-Mikal was my best man, Her daughter Lauren was her maid of honor and my **Ride or Die** Joselyn forever present at pivotal moments in my life. Two families became one as there are no "Steps" in the Alexander Household. Hell we all look the same anyway.

My step-daughter, Lauren M. Coleman:
However, in the Alexander Household,
we don't do step anything. Once I
married your mom, you became my
daughter.

January 2012: At my retirement dinner with my two favorite ladies. The next morning we left Scott Air Force Base, IL headed for our life together in NC.

In route to NC, I made a stop in Nashville, TN to meet a guy by the name of Dave Whitley. Through a series of events and synchronicity, my martial arts teacher Grandmaster Rob Williams introduced me to Dave via email. Dave is also known as the Iron Tamer and is a professional speaker and Olde Time Strong Man from the Vaudeville Era. He bends horseshoes, tears playing cards and does other things that require superhuman strength and belief to achieve. About one year before meeting Dave, I was watching a show on the SCI-FI channel called Stan Lee's Super humans. One episode had a gentleman by the name of Dennis Rodgers. Dennis is a Grandmaster Olde Time Strongman in the lineage of Joseph Greenstein the Mighty Atom.

These are some the strongest men on the planet in this photo with me:
Left to Right: Mike the Machine Bruce, me, Grandmaster Dennis Rodgers, Iron Tamer Dave Whitley.

I watched in awe as Dennis bent wrenches, rolled frying pans into scrolls among other seemingly impossible feats of strength. Now, fast forward one year. Two days before I was going to leave Scott Air Force Base and head to NC, I talked to Dave on the phone. I told him that at first, I thought he was the guy on Stan Lee's Super humans. Dave stated that Dennis was his teacher. By this time, I was a master level martial artist along with being a master level chi Kung and meditation instructor. Dave wanted to learn what I had to teach, and I wanted to learn how to bend horseshoes. That night, a deal was stuck, and we have been student teacher, teacher student and close friends ever since that moment. Dave and I also share the same birthday of November 23. I think that is the coolest thing. I taught the Iron Tamer my meditation and Chi Kung system, and he put me on the path of the Olde Time Strong Man.

Me and Grandmaster Dennis Rogers in early 2018. It was only a few short years ago that I watched Pop on Stan Lee's Superhumans doing the seemingly impossible.

Now I am bending horseshoes, snapping bats, breaking chains, tearing decks of cards, bending spikes, and driving nails through boards with my hands. I am now considered Superhuman. **Juju Who?** The impossible is only impossible because someone has told us that it is, and we believed them. The beautiful thing about the feats of strength other than watching people's eyes look on in wonder is that you can take the mindset it takes to accomplish these feats and apply them in other areas of your life. When someone at work tells me a task they have to accomplish is impossible, I sort of look at them funny and remind them to whom they are talking about what can't be done. Don't limit your thinking; you are capable of so much more.

I assumed that retirement would be fun, but after a week, I knew that I still had a lot to offer to people and sitting on the porch screaming at the school bus drivers because they are speeding through the neighborhood was not for me (yet). When I completed my graduate degree in 2005, I thought that

I was done with my formal education. However, in late 2011 after I knew my military career was over, I started thinking about earning my doctorate. I applied to Walden University in January of 2012 for the Doctor of Business Administration, specializing Leadership Track, and was accepted into the program. In February 2012 I was online looking for jobs when I noticed a position for a Health Treatment Administrator at the North Carolina Correctional Institution for Women in Raleigh, NC. As I read the position description, I realized that this is precisely what I had done as a Naval Officer. I applied for the position not knowing what to expect because it was a prison. I interviewed well, and the more I talked with the interview panel, the more I realized that I wanted that job. My last two bosses at USTRANSCOM, Dr. Lawrence Riddles, and LTCOL Heidi Hastings provided me with great references. The rest is history, and in July of 2012, I started my new career as the Head of Health Services at the North Carolina Correctional Institution for Women in charge of overseeing the provision of health services for the female offender population. For the first time in my career, I had two personal assistants, and a staff of about 280 individuals to include physicians, psychiatrists, dentists, psychologists, and others who I was responsible for serving and providing them what they needed so they could serve our special patient population. **Haha!** I had landed on my feet yet again! First when I was passed over not making Chief Petty Officer only to become a Commissioned Officer, and now after mandatory retirement from the Navy, I had now become one of the senior members in the North Carolina Department of Public Safety Health Services Division and a member of the Board of Directors. I traded the uniform of a military professional for the three-piece suits of the executive. I contacted Dr. Riddles and LTCOL Hastings thanking them for all of their support and for their references. My next career had begun. Prison Administrators from all over the United States and the world have come to see how my people conduct prison healthcare operations. My people are the best at what they do, and I am passionate about the business of correctional healthcare. Over the past six years from the writing of this book, I have become a subject matter expert on female prison healthcare operations and was actually paid to consult on a correctional healthcare project. Prison organizational structure is quasi-military. However, as I quickly learned, it is not the military. Yet, my military experience and training has served me very well. I can near instantaneously analyze a situation and develop a course of action (Rapid Response Planning Process). I do make quick decisions; I need to make certain that I get my staff to buy into the decision because it is not the military. I thank all of my past leaders on the Enlisted, Officer, and Civil Servant sides who mentored and taught me what it means to be a leader. My very first meeting with my Medical Executive Staff was interesting. I modeled my session from those that I had been a part of throughout my military career. My meetings were prompt, orderly with an agenda, and they rarely last longer than an hour. Knowing that I was an intense individual and that it could be overwhelming or intimidating, I advised my staff: *"I can be intense and go from zero to 100 in the span of a few seconds. With the best of intentions, I will march us off the cliff thinking that I am doing the right thing if you all don't stop me. If I am doing something wrong, I depend on you all to tell me."* The pink shirts and other bright colors and my love of laughter help me be **LESS** intimidating so that I am approachable, and my people and the inmates tell me their issues. However, that **switch** has been stuck in the on position for years and it is who I am; always be true to yourself.

I love the Martial Arts. The first and second
Grandmasters of Hoshin standing in the shadows.

On my way to work at the prison. The only thing that changed was the uniform

In other interactions individuals in positions of authority working for me have come to understand that I don't tolerate bullying especially from supervisors. There was one instance where I found out that one of the physicians was screaming at one of the more junior personnel who happened to work **directly** for me. I *educated* the physician: *"At the NCCIW Healthcare Facility, physicians don't yell at the help. If you are having personal issues, that is your problem. Once you take those issues out on one of my people, it automatically becomes my problem."* The physician understood my point, and that has never occurred again. I don't do bullying. I do have to check myself from time to time to make sure that I don't overreact because I know me; self-awareness is a vital leadership trait. The Medical Director, Director of Nursing and I are responsible for the healthcare mission at NCCIW, and I relay upon them to help manage me. I consult with them frequently to make certain that I am making the best decisions for the organization. If I ever get full of myself and go off the reservation, the Warden and my other Boss at the Health Services Division are there to restrain me and bring me back down to earth; the system is designed that way.

The conference room inside of the Prison Hospital that I manage. This is where I conduct the periodic staff meetings with the Executive Medical Team. Pretty good for the inside of a prison.

I strive to manage justly, and objectively. I am often the voice for individuals who feel that they can't be heard. I also encourage people to work out their differences and empower them to do so. I should only be directly involved in disputes once it becomes disruptive to the operations. Interestingly enough, I love my job at the prison. It is nearly identical to my career when I was an officer sans the deployments. Through a stroke of fate, preparedness, and luck, I am working at what would be considered a Navy Captain (O-6) level with the North Carolina Department of Public Safety. I parlayed what I learned in the military into the most interesting, fun and fascinating job I have ever had, and I am still serving the American public. This patient population is hidden away from the general public and is an underserved portion of society. One of my duties besides providing healthcare is to assist in rehabilitating these ladies in the hope that they will become productive members of society; saving the world, one person at a time.

June 2016 I completed my Doctorate with my number one fan by my side every step of the way.

In June of 2012, I begin my Doctoral Studies, and in June of 2016, I graduated with a Doctor of Business Administration, with a final GPA of 4.00. That was an exercise in endurance, patience, and persistence. People from virtually every continent on the planet have read and studied my published dissertation. My transformation was complete; Mr. Alexander was now Dr. Alexander. Any remnants of that middle school student were dead forever as I now served as an example of what others could obtain no matter the odds, obstacles, or circumstances in their lives or their past. I may not be the smartest, but my past experiences have trained me to be relentless and to never give up hope. Not every battle is worth fighting, but if I fall five times, I will get up six. Failure is only possible once you stop trying. I will give everything that I have to lift up those around me and take them on my journey so that they can eventually find their own journey if that is their desire. If you work for the benefit of others as well as yourself, rarely will you need to worry about your survival. This is not a zero sum game as there is enough success, joy, purpose, and power to go around for everyone.

In June of 2015, I had to perform one final duty wearing my Naval Officer's Uniform and that was to deliver the oath of enlistment to my oldest child, my son, James-Mikal Alexander. The cool thing about being a retired Naval Officer is that you still get to wear the good-looking uniform, without all of the hassle that comes with being on active duty.

My last official duty wearing the uniform: In June of 2015, three years after my retirement, I would deliver the oath of enlistment to my oldest, James-Mikal Alexander. The family business would continue as a second generation sailor was born.

In October of 2016, I began a part-time position as an Adjunct Professor teaching Healthcare Management Courses at the University of Maryland University College. I am training the next group of Healthcare Administrators in management and also providing my years of experience and the missteps that I have taken. I have come a long way. I provide not only examples in the literature on how to be an effective administrator, I have also provided real life examples to augment what is contained in the peer reviewed journals. Additionally, I provide prison healthcare examples because most people **(similar to me years ago)** have no experience dealing with corrections. I love teaching and watching my students grow in their own ways. Not bad for that D and F student from so many years ago.

Yes, bullying is destructive but similar to the mythological phoenix, you can rise from the ashes of that destruction and live a life of joy, purpose, and power; it merely starts with the belief that you can.

CHAPTER 7

Epilogue

I formed my company, J. Xander-Cole, Limitless, LLC in February 2018 as a response to the bullying epidemic occurring in the communities throughout the United States, and because of the events in my youth that put me on the path that I now walk. One only has to turn on the news or read a headline about a tragic event related to bullying. My goal is to empower people who feel that they have no power. I am not only passionate about meeting the needs of our youth, some adults have been bullied and are struggling to move past the memories of their ordeals. I have dedicated my life to opposing bullying and abusive behaviors by helping others improve so that they could overcome their self-imposed limitations and truly live their lives. I have done this by continuously working to improve myself as a human being, using my life as an example, and serving others. I believe that if an individual is going to speak of overcoming limitations, they should be able to use their example as the blueprint. If you can relate to people, provide them hope, and a way to move forward, you have a recipe for success.

Me with Professional Speaker, Dr. Kevin Snyder. I twisted that horse shoe and presented it to him at the conclusion of a class he taught on getting paid for public speaking.

CHAPTER 8

Five Principles for Overcoming Bullying and Self-Imposed Limitations

DISCLAIMER:

Nothing in this book is meant to serve as medical or mental health advice and I am presenting these principles with some assumptions in mind: (1) You have removed yourself from danger and sought help from a competent authority figure, (2) you have requested or will seek medical attention if it is needed, (3) you will seek mental health assistance if required, and (4), you have been cleared by a competent medical provider prior to commencing in any exercise regimen. Take what is useful to you and discard everything else. Now go forth, conquer, and achieve greatness!

Bullying is a damaging phenomenon that affects 1000s of people every year, and it took me years to realize that we never truly get over our past demons. However, we can learn to rise above our pain and live meaningful lives. I have five principles that I developed over a period of years that I used to mitigate the aftereffects of bullying to live a fufilled life.

I. **Acknowledge how bullying has adversely affected your life as this is the first step in healing.** For years, I tried to suppress the memories of my ordeal which delayed me in processing my emotions and deal with my past.

- Without necessarily reliving the specifics of the event or series of bullying events, list out all of the hurtful emotions that you have experienced as a result of bullying. Feel free to use the space below or jot down your feelings down on a separate sheet of paper.

✓ *For me, I felt shame, despair, depression, anxiety, fear, hate, anger, hopelessness*

_____

_____

_____

_____

_____

✓ **Describe in writing, how these negative emotions affected your life:**

- Withdrawn, brooding, pulled back from attention, hesitant, fearful of taking chances, scared of making mistakes, subpar grade performance, damaged relationships, unhealthy obsession with individuals ridiculing me (real or imagined)

_____

_____

_____

_____

_____

II.   Learn to forgive others as well as yourself

- While this principle has a spiritual connotation, especially among the world's dominant religions, there is a practical application to forgiving. As you contemplate this principle, reflect on the first principle and how your life has been affected:

- I learned over the years, that forgiveness has everything to do about you and very little about the tormentor. Often that individual has moved on in their lives while we continuously give them power over our lives by holding onto these experiences

- Holding onto anger and all of those hurtful emotions is the equivalent to continually drinking poison and hoping that the individual(s) who hurt you will get sick when in actuality you are the only one getting poisoned. I wasted years remaining angry while reliving the 6th grade. I often wondered how much more I could have accomplished at this stage in my life if it hadn't taken me years to truly forgive and move on.

- This process is simple but not easy. True forgiveness rarely occurs overnight. However, if you give up the hope for a better past and make a commitment to work on forgiving a little each day, you can learn to forgive.

- Use the below space or a separate sheet of paper to write down your thoughts and feelings on forgiveness and how you learning to forgive will help you move on.

_____

_____

_____

_____

_____

- The bullying was not your fault and being a victim was not your fault.

- Self-Forgiveness is the beginning of healing.

- Forgive yourself for blaming yourself for being victimized.

- Bullying is the weak person's imitation of strength, and they seek. to prey on those who they perceive as weak.

- We just happened to be a target of opportunity at the time, and there was very little that we could have done to prevent it.

- In retrospect, confronting the issue and either addressing it directly as soon as it occurred may have stopped it sooner, but this is hindsight; asking for help from my teachers did not help as back then they were only words.

- Use the space below to write down your thoughts on how learning to forgive yourself will help you move on with your life.

_____

_____

_____

_____

_____

III. Talk to someone about your experiences

- Someone you trust or a Professional Therapist.

- The very process of speaking about your experiences loosens the power that bullying has over your life.

- Talking about your experiences can be cathartic and help in processing your emotions.

- Talking to someone about your ordeal is getting the poison out of you so that you can heal.

- I didn't talk about my experiences in detail until many years later in front of a group of strangers at a Toast Masters meeting and was the subject of my 1st speech, and the very process was empowering.

- In the space below, write down the names of some people that you trust and can talk with about your experiences.

_____

_____

_____

_____

_____

IV.   Take care of your body, mind, and spirit

- A Strong Body leads to a keen mind and strong spirit.

- When you are healthy, you give off a vibe of confidence as you feel better about yourself.

- When you are strong, you can better handle the stresses of daily living.

- When you are confident, you decrease the likelihood of being a victim.

- When you feel good about yourself, you are less likely to victimize others.

- Studies have demonstrated that the feel-good hormones, endorphins, serotonin, and dopamine are released post exercise.

- After getting cleared by your medical provider, pick an exercise and diet regimen that you can commit to for the rest of your life; something that you find enjoyable.

- Always try to improve on whatever you have decided to pursue.

- Take pride in the fact that you have made a life-altering decision that can yield positive effects.

- The below activities have worked for me over my lifetime. Find what works for you:

- Martial Arts

- Strength Training

- Kettle bell Training

- Mace bell Training

- Yoga

- Oldetime Feats of Strength Training

- In the space below, write out some physical activities that you find enjoyable. Once you are cleared by your medical provider, let's get with it and commit to a regimen!

_____

_____

_____

_____

_____

_____

_____

✓ Continue your education formally and informally by becoming a lifelong learner. There is something empowering about learning new topics and being able to talk intelligently about them. Although I have completed my formal education, I continue to educate and work on improving myself by:

- Taking Classes at the community college.

- Khan's Academy to learn numerous subjects ranging from healthcare to statistics.

- Big History Project which blends history and science together.

- Toastmasters to practice your public speaking skills in a non-threatening environment.

- Free online classes at some of the United States Ivy League Universities.

- Once you become competent on a subject, teach it to people so that it solidifies your learning.

- Use the space below to write down ways that you are going to commit to being a lifelong learner:

_____

_____

_____

_____

_____

✓ Reading: My late friend and teacher Dr. Glenn Morris often stated that readers are leaders, and I love to read. I have an untold number of Kindle Books, E-Books, Hard Back Books and Paper Back Books. This exercises your creativity and imagination. It also increases your knowledge which can increase your confidence:

- Fiction

- Non-Fiction

- History

- Science

- Comic Books

- Leadership

- Philosophy

- Autobiographies

- Use the space below to write down some books that you always wanted to read and then commit to reading those books:

_____

_____

_____

_____

_____

✓ Find a spiritual practice that resonates with you and commit to it.

• Your practices can help to calm your spirit to the point that you can remain calm and exude that calmness in most situations.

• If conducted properly, you learn to slow your thoughts and control your emotions through your spiritual practices.

• Positive Affirmations: Look into the mirror and speak positively to yourself. Affirmations are crucial to killing the negative self-talk.

• Practice Positive Body Language: As your body language is tied to your limbic system, it can reveal how a person is feeling. Conversely, your body language can influence how you feel.

• Meditation: Can help in quieting your mind and process your experiences.

- Breathing Practices: Once you learn how to control your breathing, you can begin to control your thoughts and emotions.

- Chi Kung or Tai Chi.

- Smile and Laugh Often: I love to laugh, and once I overcame my trauma, I begin laughing a lot more. There is something therapeutic about laughing and laughing at yourself. You learn to not take yourself too serious.

- Go out into the sun and enjoy your life! We live a short time on this planet, and one day it will be over; so get out and make the most of every moment. It is your life, and you have the power to create the life that you desire.

- Use the space below to write out how you will implement and integrate this final principle into your life:

_____

_____

_____

_____

_____

V. Take a stance against bullying

- Getting involved in an anti-bullying or youth organization.

- Speaking out against bullying when you observe it.

- Befriend and mentor a person who has been bullied.

- Share your story with the anticipation that it will help somebody.

- Use the space below and write down the ways that you will take a stance against bullying.

_____

_____

_____

_____

_____

As you can see within the context of five principles, I have included a blueprint for addressing the needs of your mind, body, and spirit. It is only when these three aspects of yourself are positively unified that you can leave your limitations behind, reach for greatness and accomplish the impossible. Now go forth and conquer and achieve greatness!

About the Author

Dr. James F. Alexander is a native of Oklahoma City, OK and is a retired United States Navy Veteran with over 23 years of military service. He began his service to the United States in November of 1988 when he enlisted in the United States Navy as a Hospital Corpsman. In 2001, Dr. Alexander was commissioned as a Naval Office into the Medical Service Corps as a Healthcare Administrator, and in April of 2012, he retired from the Navy. In July of 2012, Dr. Alexander began a new career with the North Carolina Department of Public Safety as the Healthcare Facility Chief Executive Officer at the North Carolina Correctional Institution for Women in Raleigh, NC. Dr. Alexander became an Anti-bullying advocate because of countless traumatic events covered in the news media, and after reflecting on a period of bullying that occurred in his youth which impacted his life. He has used his life's story as an example to demonstrate that you can overcome past hurts and turmoil to live a life of purpose, joy, and power. As a public speaker, Dr. Alexander incorporates feats of strength such:

- Bending Spikes

- Twisting Horseshoes,

- Tearing Decks of Cards

- Driving Nails through Boards with his hand

- Breaking Baseball Bats in Two

- Breaking Chains

Dr. Alexander utilizes his strength performance along with his personal story to illustrate what is possible, and that overcoming the seemingly insurmountable is feasible; it starts with a thought and desire, followed up with a relentless effort to conquer your past victimhood to live life on your terms. His motto is Numquid Victims Non, which is Latin for Victims no Longer.

With his personal story of tragedy, death, and rebirth, he hopes to inspire and empower those who have been shackled by bullying, and other past hurts to break free of self-imposed limitations to achieve greatness. Dr. Alexander can be contacted for speaking engagments at 919-438-3509, and at jxandercolelimitlessllc@gmail.com. Please connect with him on Linkedin: https://www.linkedin.com/in/dr-james-fitzgerald-alexander-dba-mba-bs-425a1913/.

Notes

Notes

Notes

Notes

Notes

Notes

Made in the USA
Columbia, SC
12 January 2019